TrainingDirector
TIPS

Openers & Closers
For Meetings

Published by Bardolf & Company

Openers and Closers for Meetings

ISBN 978-1-938842-35-7

For information write:

    Bardolf & Company
    5430 Colewood Pl.
    Sarasota, FL 34232
    941-232-0113

Printed in the United States of America

Cover design by Janine Giovinazzi, dzine studio

Training Doctor
TIPS

Openers & Closers
For Meetings

Geri McArdle Ph.D.

Bardolf & Company
Sarasota, Florida

CONTENTS

INTRODUCTION

Over the past 20 years in my career as a business consultant and corporate trainer, I have held a lot of meetings and led numerous workshops. Along the way, I figured out the three secret ingredients to conducting a successful event every time. They have worked equally well in the United States and in places like Saudi Arabia where I spent considerable time.

The components are:

1. Immediately engaging the audience
2. Focusing the meeting content around a theme
3. Providing an audience takeaway

This book is a collection of openers and closers that address all three. While the terms "openers" and "closers" might seem self-explanatory, I want to share my definitions, as well as some strategies to use to create your own meeting activities.

Openers

Meeting openers are activities usually used by a leader to facilitate meetings, presentations, workshops, training seminars, and education programs in a wide variety of settings.

These include student and teacher training, from elementary to secondary schools, managerial training in business and corporate venues, and work in therapeutic and /or correctional institutions.

Another term often used for them is "icebreakers." There are many different types of openers or icebrakers. Here are three common types:

Introductory: Use an introductory icebreaker game or activity to help people begin to know each other. An introductory icebreakers can be simple, such as, asking each person to tell the group their name or a complicated activity designed to establish trust and a desire to work together.

Team building: Use a team building icebreaker to improve group dynamics and increase the participants' enthusiasm and energy. Team building activities can be fun while others can be complex tasks designed and executed for specific reasons.

Party (Fun): Use a party icebreaker to introduce guests to one another. The party activities can be a simple fun game or a complex task designed for a specific reason.

Closer

Closers are what bring the meeting or workshop to conclusion and should review what was accomplished. The ending is important because audience remember what you said last. That is way the way you create the closing will define their future attitude toward what they have learned.

How to use this book and create your own activities

- Once you know the size of your group and the materials you need, decide how much time you have. Most openers are short, including the time to process what happened, so that the bulk of your meeting can be spent on the material you wish to cover.

- Decide if your audience members will appreciate warming up by talking with each other or if they are more action oriented and will appreciate engaging in physical movement. In cases where the people know each other already, they will not want to waste their time with a "getting to know you" activity.

- Next, determine a concept relative to the meeting topic. It should be engaging, worthy of reinforcement, potentially expandable, and likely to spark discussion.

I also recommend that you practice ahead of time, conducting "dry run" for yourself to avoid surprises. It's amazing how much can go wrong, from easels falling over to marking pens not workings. While a good sense of humor will usually get you past such obstacles, you will encounter fewer if you practice the activity ahead of time and make it your own.

Ultimately, it's about having fun. People who enjoy themselves relax and become more receptive to what you have to teach.

I wish you success and encourage you to provide me with feedback via my website, *www.http://trainingdoctor.u*s.

I'd like to thank Chris Angermann of Bardolf & Company for helping me get this book to publication.

Geri McArdle, Ph.D.
Ft. Myers, Florida 2017

OPENERS

ALPHABET SOUP

Opener

Materials

None

Directions

- Break the class into teams or groups.

- Ask each team to gather personal items (from the table, their pockets, purses etc.) that represent each letter of the alphabet.

- Place the objects in the middle of your table.

- Everyone stand when finished (maximum time—5 minutes).

- When time is up or when first team stands, ask them to identify each item by letter.

- Debriefing questions: Was a leader identified? How? Was a plan developed? What would you do differently? Why?

Comment

Introduces group dynamics and group roles.

ALTER EGO

Opener

Materials

Name Tents or Nametags

Directions

- Ask participants to put their name on their name tent or nametag along with the name of their alter ego. Example: CowardlyLion, Albert Einstein, Napoleon.

- When they are introducing themselves, ask them to explain why they chose their alter ego.

Comment

A good opportunity to explore self in fun way.

DIFFERENCES

Opener

Materials

None

Directions

- Divide participants into pairs.

- Ask them to work with their partners to list the differences between them—hair, eye color, education, state of birth, etc.

- Ask them to introduce each other using their differences.

- Award the pair with the longest list a prize.

Comment

This activity is useful for establishing group trust early on.

FANTASY OCCUPATION

Opener

Materials

None

Directions

- Ask participants to invent a fantasy occupation for themselves.
- Then ask them to introduce themselves, and tell about their jobs and job responsibilities.

Alternative

Make up fantasy occupations and ask participants to choose one.

Sample Occupations

Knitting, Needle Sharpener, Apple Polisher, Jelly Bean Counter, Greeting Card Folder, Candy Bar Wrapper.

Comment

Great for making discussion points, exploring how we make choices and practicing story telling.

GUESS WHO

Opener

Materials

3 X 5 cards

Directions

- As participants enter the class, ask them to complete 3 X 5 card with the following information:

  - Their favorite type of food
  - Their favorite all time TV show
  - The last movie they saw
  - The last book they read
  - Their dream vacation

- After they'v signed their names, gather all cards.

- During the class, read the cards and ask the group to guess who the person being described is.

Comment

This works best with groups that "think" they know each other well.

I'M UNIQUE

Opener

Materials

None

Directions

As part of making their introductions, ask participants to share something about themselves which makes them unique.

Comment

This provides a quick way to establish group member support.

LABEL YOURSELF

Opener

Materials

None

Directions

- As participants introduce themselves to the class, ask them to identify if they are

  - prisoners,
  - exlorers, or
  - vacationers,

  and explain why they picked their labels.

Comment

This is a quick way to gauge how willing the group is to engage and commit.

MOVIE LINE QUOTES

Opener

Materials

Easel pad paper

Directions

- Put sheets of paper on the wall.

- Ask participants to read and post a quote on the paper during their introductions.

- The task is to try to work the quotes into the discussion during the class. Whoever manages to do so gets a prize.

- As a quote is used, remove it from the paper on the wall.

Comments

This activity provides the group with an early opportunity to engage in an easily focused task.

HELLO EVERYBODY

Opener

Materials

None

Directions

- The first person introduces himself/herself with, "Hello, everybody, my name is Ted." (example)

- The second person says, "Hello, Ted, my name is Bob."

- The third person would say, "Hello, Ted and Bob, my name is Mary."

- Continue until everyone has introduced him/herself in this way.

- Everyone gets to greet each other and hears everyone's name repeated enough times to hopefully remember most of the group.

Comments

This exercise is a fast way to learn group names.

HUMAN LETTERS

Opener

Materials

None

Directions

- Divide class into 3 to 6 teams. Identify a word (or words) used in the training. Explain that you are going to spell the word _____. When you point to a team, its members must all form the letters, using everyone on the team.

- Continue to point to all teams randomly and let them scramble to form the letters.

- Process the activity.

Comment

An energizing activity that is also good for team building.

NAME TAG SWITCH

Opener

Materials

Name tags

Directions

- Give each participant someone else's nametag and tell them each to find the person on the tag—by whatever means necessary.

- Everyone should meet at least 2 people, the person who they have to find, and the person who finds them.

Comment

This game can be confusing but it is a great way to get to know some of the people in a group who don't know each other.

ROPE SQUARE

Opener

Materials

A rope about 25 feet long
Bandanas or blindfolds for each

Directions

- Place the rope on the floor in a loose circle. Ask the group to make a circle around the rope. Everyone must keep their eyes closed. If you open them you must leave the game so it is better and easier to just put on blindfolds.

- When the group leader says go, they put on your blindfolds. Everyone will find, touch and pick up the rope.

- They have 5 minutes to create a perfect square with the rope.

- Rules: Everyone must continue to touch the rope at all times.

- When you say stop, everyone will lay down the rope and take off the blindfolds.

- Discuss and process the activity.

Comment

This is a good exercise for team building and encouraging creative thinking. For a group of 12-15 people; the facilitator will ensure that everyone will be safe.

THIS IS ME!

Opener

Materials

3 X 5 cards

Directions

- Give participants a 3 by 5 card.

- Ask them to write the answer to each of these questions. What is your favorite

  - What is your favorite—Color Car
  - Character (real or fictional)
  - Cuisine
  - Holiday movie
  - Desire

- When everyone has finished, gather the cards, shuffle them and, as you read them, ask the group to guess who wrote them. After everyone has guessed, ask the real person to stand.

Comment

This exercise works well with groups that think they know each other well.

BALL TOSS

Opener

Materials

Two soft balls

Directions

- Create 2 teams. Give each team a ball.

- Participants have to say the name of the person to whom they toss the ball. Everyone gets to toss and receive the ball once.

- When all paticipants have finished tossing and receiving the ball—tell them to do it again in the "same order only faster."

- The object of the final round is to do it the fastest way. The only rules are: do it in the same order and everyone must touch the ball.

- Process the activity: How didyou feel as the rounds sped up? What creative solutions did you find? What were the biggest challenges? Does everyone know each other's names?

Comment

Good for team building, especially groups that don't know each other well.

CARD DRAW

Opener

Materials

Deck of cards
Prizes

Directions

- Give each participant a playing card from the deck. (If you have more than 52 people in your group, add additional decks as needed.)

- Tell them that they have 3 minutes to find four partners and introduce themselves.

- The group of 5 with the best "hand" wins a prize (like a deck of cards for each of them!).

Comment

Discuss that this exercise shows that learning observation skills is important.

SILLY HATS

Opener

Materials

Piece of newspaper/newprint per participant

Directions

- Have participants to fold their paper into a hat.

- Announce, "This is the worst thing that can happen to you today! I thought we would get it out of the way so we don't have to worry about it and can get on with the training."

- Ask participants to model their hats and stand and introduce themselves to the group.

Comment

A good opportunity to feel comfortable with being a group member.

WHAT'S IN A NAME

Opener

Materials

Paper
Pen/Pencil

Directions

- Distribute handouts. Ask participants to write their name vertically in a "thought bubble."

- Then ask them to write a positive word or short phrase to describe themselves using each letter in their name.

- When introducing themselves, ask them to finish with the words from the letters in their names.

- For a lengthy session, post the results around the room so participants can look at them during breaks.

Comment

This activity helps participants remember each others' names.

LEARNING WORDS

Opener

Materials

Easel pad paper
Masking tape markers of different colors

Directions

- Label one piece of pad paper with "Learning" and another piece with "Words."

- Tape the pad papers on opposite walls in the room and provide several different color markers for each chart.

- Participants go to the pad papers and write one thing they want to find out during the workshop on the "Learning" paper and one thing they want to share with the group on the "Words" pad paper.

- Before everyone leaves, review what is written on both papers with the group.

- You may choose to take the charts and create documents to share with the participants.

Comment

This activity can be used to both open and close the session (see page 83).

UP FRONT QUESTIONS

Opener

Materials

Easel pad paper
Large sticky notes

Directions

- Introduce the topic: "The purpose of this activity is to find out what we know and don't know about _____" (whatever the workshop is for).

- Put 4 large sheets of pad paper on the wall and label them:

    - What I know about _____ (workshop name)
    - Questions I have about _____
    - Websites/Books/Journals that are good for _____
    - How I define _____

- Give participants large sticky notes and ask them to write as many answers as they can and then attach their notes on the corresponding sheet on the wall.

- Bring the group back together and discuss the information gathered and then transition into the workshop.

Comment

This activity is a good way to explore the theme and topics of the workshop.

STICKER INTRODUCTIONS

Opener

Materials

Pairs of stickers or decals.

Directions

- Put one of each pair at each place setting.

- As participants enter, hand them each a sticker and ask them to find the place setting with the matching sticker and sit there.

- Then ask them to find out:
    - The name of the person to the right of them
    - How he/she got their name
    - What he/she is doing at the workshop

- Have them Introduce the person next to them to the group.

Comment

Great group mixer and a needs assessment process.

WALLET SEARCH

Opener

Materials

None

Directions

- Ask participants to take out their wallets and remove three items that best describe them. They may NOT choose their Driver's License or ID Card. If they pick a photograph, they can use only one.

- Ask them to pair up with someone in the group whom they do not know, or don't know well, and share the items.

- Each pair then shares their conversation with the group as introductions are made.

Comment

A creative way for the members to the group to meet and get to know each other.

NAME TAGS INTRO

Opener

Materials

> 5 name tags per participant
> Markers

Directions

- Give every participant five name tags and a marker.

- Give the following instructions: Complete the five name tags for yourself identifying these categories:
    - your name
    - Where you work
    - How long have you worked there
    - Where you are from
    - Your favorite cookie

- Put all 5 of the name tags on you.

- Move around the room and silently introduce yourself using only the name tags and body language!

Variation

Use different categories for the name tags.

Comment

A fast "get to know you" exercise.

FLORIDA LANDMARKS

Opener

Materials

None

Directions

- Stand in the middle of the room and declare that the spot you occupy represents Disney World in Orlando, Florida.

- Ask participants to position themselves around the room depending on where they live in relation to Disney World.

- Ask participants to speak to their closest neighbor and tell them where there is a good nearby
  - bakery
  - restaurant
  - movie theater
  - public park
  - shopping mall

- Repeat the exercise with another "neighbor."

Comment

If the workshop is being held in a different state, pick a recognizable local landmark or attraction.

FAVORITE FOOD

Opener

Materials

Easel pad paper hung on the walls around the room, showing different types of food
Markers

Directions

- Ask participants to choose their favorite food and go to that chart.

- Instruct the groups to introduce themselves, discuss their choice, and decide why their food is the best in the room.

- Have them write the reasons on the chart pages.

- After 10 minutes, ask the groups to introduce the group members and explain the reasons why their food choice is the best.

Variations

Instead of food, use music, types of vacations, types of transportation, etc.

Comment

Breaks barriers as people seek and develop common bonds.

DUELING EASELS

Opener

Materials

Tape
Easel
Newsprint paper

Directions

- Divide the group into 2 teams.

- Draw a line on the floor and place an easel with newsprint on each side of the line. Teams line up on each side of the line.

- Ask them to brainstorm and develop a strategy or activity to make as many crossings as possible in 30 seconds. Only 1 person from each team at a time can go.

- Each team should make a list of possible ways of meeting the goal, pick one, and then try to execute it in turn.

- Discuss and process the activity.

Comment

This exercise is great for team building and encouraging creative thinking.

PAPER AIRPLANES

Opener

Materials

Paper
Masking tape

Directions

- Draw a line across the floor. Give participants each a piece of paper. Explain that they are to construct an airplane "to fly the farthest that it will go."

- The only rule is that they must stand behind the line.

- Allow 5 minutes.

- Discuss and process the activity. Include comment such as, "I never said that the object was to see whose plane goes the farthest." "What did you learn from this activity?" "What rules did you impose upon yourself?"

Comment

This activity is great for exploring how well people listen to directions, and whether or not they ask clarifying questions.

ACCEPTANCE SPEECH

Opener

Materials

None

Directions

- Ask the participants to introduce themselves and thank someone who has contributed to their professional development. They should thank the person as if they were receiving an Academy Award.

- After everyone has had a turn, discuss how verbal and nonverbal a skills are important.

Comment

Caution: you may have to limit the speeches to 30 seconds!

Takeaway: always be ready with your elevator speech.

SCREAM THERAPY

Opener

Materials

None

Directions

- Ask participants to introduce themselves and share an emotion they feel about dealing with a difficult person or customer. (Example: "They drive me nuts!")

- Have them say it with FEELING!

- At the end of the introductions, have them all scream the feelings at the same time.

Comment

Caution: this activity can get noisy!

CHARADES

Opener

Materials

None

Directions

- Break the group into small teams. Ask them to identify one type of person they all find difficult.

- Ask each team to act out the type of behavior they identified while the rest of the class tries to guess what they are portraying.

- Process what happened.

Comment

This is a fun activity that can lead to a good discussion about needing to keep a sense of humor when dealing with people.

LEARNING FROM EXPERIENCE

Opener

Materials

Easel
Easel pad

Directions

- Ask participants to introduce themselves and explain one thing they have learned the hard way about the topic of your class.

- Post the "learnings" on the easel pad and refer to them throughout the session.

Comment

This is a good way to introduce and discuss the idea how past experiences matter.

SPINNING A YEARN

Opener

Materials

Ball of bright colored yarn

Directions

- Gather the group into a circle. The leader holds the ball of yarn, shares something interesting about him/herself. Holding the end of the yarn, toss the ball to another person—who repeats the process.

- Continue until everyone is holding the yarn and a web is formed within the circle.

- Everyone is responsible to keep the yarn taut. At the end, with total cooperation, the web must be untangled and the ball rewound.

Comment

Great with kids.

THE COLORS GAME

Opener

Materials

Colored candies like M&Ms or Skittles
Flip chart with color code

Directions

- Ask participants to each take 3 different colored candies. After they all have their candies,
explain that they need to state their name
and provide information about themselves,
based on the color of the candies they selected.

    - Dark brown–your favorite TV show
    - Light Brown–your favorite movie this year
    - Yellow–your favorite sport
    - Red–your favorite singer/or song
    - Blue–your favorite vacation
    - Green–your favorite fast food
    - Orange–yYour favorite book

- Process the individual answers.

Comment

This activity provides a great opportunity for
asking questions; plus, it's fun.

I, ME, MY

Opener

Materials

Supply of small items such as beans, beads, peanuts or candies

Directions

- Give out 10 items to each participant. Ask the group to converse and mingle.

- Whenever someone says the words, "I", "Me", or "My," he or she must give a bean or bead to the person they're talking with.

- Whoever is able to get others to open up about themselves and has the most beans in 5 minutes wins.

Comment

This exercise emphasizes the art of listening.

WHO AM I

Opener

Materials

Stick on name tags

Directions

- In advance, pick a category that the group will relate to.

- Let's use cartoons for our example. Write one cartoon character's name on a name tag for each participant.

- To play, place one of the name tags on each person's back. Everyone now asks questions of the others (with a yes or no answer only) to identify their character.

- Once they have guessed correctly, they can move the tag to the front.

Comment

This is a good mix and mingle activity and you can use groups of names to form small teams. (for example: The Flintstones.)

FINISH THE LINE

Opener

Materials

Slips of paper
Hat or container

Directions

- In advance, pick a category that the group will relate to. Prepare famous quotes on slips of paper. Cut each quote in half and place each paper in a container. They can be classic quotes or current phrases (for example: "Misery loves company," "Blood is thicker than water," or "Money is the root of all evil.").

- Make sure that you have the same number of slips in the container as participants.

- Ask everyone to draw a slip and find the person who has the other half of the quote.

Comment

Another good mix and mingle activity that emphasizes developing good questioning skills and creative strategies (such as shouting out one's half quote, hoping for a response).

WHOLE ROOM HANDSHAKE

Opener

Materials

None

Directions

- Have the group form into two large circles, one inside the other.

- Ask the circles to face each other and have the people opposite one another introduce themselves.

- The outer circle then continues to rotate one step to the right and the inner circle one step to the left.

- Continue introductions until everyone has met each member of the other circle.

Comment

A great way to rememer names and faces. It sharpens observation skills by emphasizing the importance watching for both nonverbal and verbal behavior cues.

TEAR IT TOGETHER

Opener

Materials

1 piece of colored paper per participant

Directions

- Distribute a piece of colored paper to each participant. Ask everyone to close their eyes.

- Ask them to fold the paper in half and tear off one corner and continue tearing until the paper is small.

- Ask everyone to open their eyes and unfold their paper.

- Show class that everyone has a different design. This leads into a discussion of how we are all unique.

Comment

This is a communication exercise, good for encouraging cultural awareness—we all do not hear the same words or instructions, resulting in the paper looking like different snowflakes.

.

BAND PRACTICE

Opener

Materials

One folded slip of paper per participant that contains the name of an instrument. (for examples: tuba, clarinet, trumpet, saxophone, triangle, etc.)

Directions

- Give each participant a slip of paper upon arrival.

- After everyone has arrived, ask the participants to stand up and "tune up" their instruments, imitating the sound their instrument makes.

- When everyone is ready, the give the group the name of the song they will be performing together (suggested songs: "Mary Had a Little Lamb," "Row, Row, Row Your Boat," "Jingle Bells").

- The group "practices" playing the song, then performs" it, with the group leader conducting.

Comment

Good icebreaker to etablish instant rapport.

HULA HOOPS

Opener

Materials

Several hula hoops

Directions

- Divide the group into two teams.
- Team members have to pass around hula hoops without using their hands until everyone has been involved.

Variation

Make it a contest and award prizes to the first team to involve all of its members.

Comment

Emphasizes the need for good team work and group leadership skills.

M&M GAME

Opener

Materials

A small bowl of M&Ms for each table

Directions

- Ask each participant to pick one M&M out of the bowl.

- When everyone has picked their candy, ask each person to introduce him or herself and explain why they picked that particular M&M.

- Most people I know love M & Ms (even if they aren't good for your diet!)

Comment

The responses will vary and open the door for discussions on differences and similarities among people, as well as the uniqueness of each person, even though they may work for the same agency, have the same profession, or are at a similar stage of life.

THE TENNIS BALL GAME

Opener

Materials

Tennis ball

Directions

- Ask the group to stand in a circle. Start the game by introducing yourself and state an important role in your daily life.

- Pass the tennis ball to another person, who introduces himself or herself and states an important role in their daily life. This continues until each person has had a turn.

- Continue passing the tennis ball. However, this time participants will pass the ball to someone else, introduce that person and state the important role in that person's life.

Comment

This exercise is a good way for participants to get to know each other in a personal way.

It's always interesting to see how many things people actually remember about others.

MULTIPLE TENNIS BALLS

Opener

Materials

Several tennis balls

Directions

- Ask the group to form a circle. The instructor stands in the middle.

- One person starts the game with a tennis ball and states an important role in his or her daily life, then passes the ball to the person on the right.

- The instructor hands that person an additional ball. That person lists two important roles in their daily life.

- The game continues with each person receiving additional tennis balls and having to list an additional role.

- It is interesting to see how far around the circle the group gets before someone is unable to hold all of the tennis balls and they fall to the ground.

Comment

This exercise demonstrates that each of us can get overwhelmed with trying to "juggle" many different roles in our lives. To prevent things eventually falling apart, we need to prioritize what is important in our daily lives and ask others to help us with the rest of our tasks.

It is also a good oppotunity to practice the art of delegating.

TRASH IT

Opener

Materials

Small trash can
Paper

Directions

- Pass out paper and ask participants to write down their most pressing problem (business or personal). Assure them that no one else will see them.

- When they are finished, collect them all. Tear them into little pieces, toss them in the trash can and move on with the class.

Comment

Great way to start a session by addressing stress and anxiety issues without any comments.

GIVE AND TAKE

Opener

Materials

    2 easels
Newsprint

Directions

- Have participants pair up and ask their partners to answer two questions:

    - What's one quality, skill, talent, etc., that you are bringing to this training?
    - What one thing do you want (expect) to take away from this training?

- Participants then introduce their partner with the answer to the two questions.

- Recorders write down the answers (suggest having 2 recorders)

Comment

This method eliminates the opportunity for an individual to give you his 'life story' and also provides you with a list of participant expectations.

ADJECTIVE INTRODUCTIONS

Opener

Materials

None

Directions

- Ask participants to introduce themselves using an adjective that begins with the first letter of their name (for example: Electric Elizabeth).

- Before they introduce themselves, they have to repeat all of the names and matching adjectives that went before them.

Comment

This is a great way for the class to learn the names of new friends.

MAROONED

Opener

Materials

Easel
Newsprint

Directions

- Divide the class into teams. Tell them that they are marooned on a deserted island. As a team, they are to agree on 5 items that they would have brought with them, if they had known their fate. List them on the newsprint.

- Ask each team to explain their choices to the rest of the class.

Comment

This activity helps the class to learn about other's values and problem solving skills, and promotes teamwork.

THE MAGIC WAND

Opener

Materials

None

Directions

- Tell the group that you have just found a magic wand that allows you to change work related activities.

- Each person will be allowed to change one thing. What would you change about yourself, your job, your program or project, etc.? Ask participants to discuss why it is important to make the change.

Variation

Ask participants what they would change if they were Boss for a day.

Comment

This activity helps the class learn about other's values and frustrations.

THE WORST TEAM

Opener

Materials

Easel
Newsprint

Directions

- Ask participants to share a description of the worst team they have ever been on and why that experience was so bad.

- List the characteristics on an easel.

- Process the activity by discussing the ways to avoid the "worst team" characteristics.

Comment

Use the list to use as a guide to remind us not to use these behaviors.

UNIQUENESS AND COMMONALITIES

Opener

Materials

None

Directions

- Form the participants into small teams and ask them to talk and share among themselves:

    - Something they all have in common (for example: all have children)
    - Something about each person that is totally unique (which pertains to no one else on the team).

- When all teams are finished, ask them to share the results with the rest of the class.

Comment

This activity provides an opportunity to relax and feel at ease with the group.

WING IT OR WAD IT

Opener

Materials

Paper
Easel

Directions

- Ask participants to anonymously write one question related to the workshop topic on a piece of paper.

- Tell them to wad the paper into a ball or make it into an airplane.

- Throw the balls and airplanes into the center of the room.

- Ask participants each to retrieve one paper and read the question out loud the class.

- Write the questions on the easel.

- Use the list of questions as a checklist during the session or as a review.

Comment

This exercise is especially good for embarrassing or sensitive subjects, such as participants not knowing anything about the subject and being afraid to ask questions.

PENNY FOR YOUR THOUGHT

Opener

Materials

Enough pennies for everyone in the class

Directions

- Place at least one penny for each of the participants into a cup. Pass the cup around the room and ask everyone to take one penny.

- When all participants have a penny, ask them to find the mint date on their penny.

- As they introduce themselves, each person will give the date on their penny and tell something memorable (personal or historical) from that year.

Comment

This exercise reveals a lot about the experiences of your participants.

OPPOSITES ATTRACT – I

Opener

Materials

None

Directions

- Bring everyone into the center of the room (or an open space).

- Explain that you are going to make a statement and, if they agree or it applies to them, they will be directed to one side of the room. If they disagree or it does not apply to them, they will go to the opposite side.

  (Examples: I welcome changes. I watch the TV show, "Game of Thrones." I am over 5 feet 10 inches tall. I was born in the USA. Statements also can be related to the workshop topic.)

- Give participants time to walk across the room if necessary before the next statement.

Comment

The object of this activity is to move around, have fun, and get to know about each other.

This activity can also be used as a closer.

CLOSERS

OPPOSITES ATTRACT - II

Closer

Materials

Paper
Pencils

Directions

- Divide participants into groups of four (or use existing groups).

- Ask each team to review the material presented and formulate 3 to 5 questions about that material.

- When the teams are finished, ask them to trade questions with the other teams.

- When all teams have exchanged questions, they are to answer the questions.

- Discuss the questions and answers with the large group (optional).

Comment

The opener asked for participants to list their wishes. The closer asks them what "takeaway" they will use after the session —a good way to summarize leanring.

BUTT WRITING

Closer

Materials

None

Directions

- Break class into several small groups.

- Each team has to think of a word, related to the training, that contains the same number of letters as there are members of the team.

- Taking turns, each team will stand with their backs to the rest of the class. Using only their backsides, each team member will "write" one letter of the word until the class guesses the word.

Comment

This exercise promotes the need for good listening skills and team work; emphasize the need for team work and task behavior.

ABC REVIEW

Closer

Materials

None

Directions

- Divide participants into teams. Make sure it's an uneven number.

- Teams will have 7 minutes to brainstorm a list of takeaways, organize the words or phrases in alphabetical order and record on chart paper.

- The goal is for each team to have something unique and different that the other teams do not have.

- When time is up, ask each team to tell what they have for each letter. Every time something on a list matches another list or lists, the teams must cross it off.

- The team with the highest number of unusual items (actually discussed during training!) is the winner.

Comment

If you play march music, it adds fun to the final review.

TICKER TAPE PARADE

Closer

Materials

Roll of adding machine tape
Markers
Masking tape

Directions

- Divide class into small groups or teams.

- Give each team about 3 yards of tape and markers.

- Ask each team to list some lessons learned in this class.

- When finished, post them up around the room and then allow participants to walk around the room and read each tape.

Comment

If you play march music it adds fun to the final review.

COMMERCIAL BREAK

Closer

Materials

Chart paper
Markers
Masking tape

Directions

- Divide participants into small groups.

- Give each group some chart paper, markers and masking tape.

- Ask them to create a 30-second commercial. The commercial should be developed so it could be "heard" on the radio or "seen" on television.

- Have each group perform in front of the whole group.

Comment

This activity serves to summarize the content hightlights of the session.

HIGH FLYING

Closer

Materials

Paper
Pencil

Directions

- At the end of the training, give each person a piece of paper, and ask them to write their names and telephone number on it.

- Ask them to write one thing they learned from the training and will begin using.

- Have each person fold their piece of paper into a paper airplane and fly it!

- Each participant should catch or find someone else's airplane.

- Each participant is asked to telephone the person whose plane they caught two weeks after the training to discuss how they have applied the idea they listed.

Comment

This activity serves to summarize the content hightlights of the session.

YOU ARE...

Closer

Materials

One set of name papers (with the names of the participants)
Tape
Stickers
Markers

Directions

- Put the names of the participants on the papers (one on each) and place them around the room.

- Give each participant some sticky labels (one for each participant).

- Ask each participant to write one of the following categories on a label for each classmate. Put the label on the piece of paper with the participant's name.

- Participants may take the papers with them.

Comment

Great takeaway exercise.

Sample Categories

Funniest person, kindest person, most out-going person, most artistic person, cleverest person, most reliable person, friendliest person, most flexible person, most trustworthy person, most fashionable person, most empathetic person, hardest working person, most perceptive person, most accepting person, wisest person, most approachable person, mMost uncritical person, smartest person, most serious person, most confident person, calmest person, most lively person, most logical person, most generous person.

PAPER TOWEL EVALUATION

Closer

Materials

One roll of paper towels (in tearable squares)
Sticky notes

Directions

- Pass the roll of paper towels around and instruct participants to "take one."

- Once they all have a paper towel ask them to count how many squares they have and tell the people on either side of them.

- Participants must list on the sticky notes one thing they have learned or reaffirmed during the training for each paper towel square they have taken.

- Go around the room and ask them to share what they've come up with.

Comment

Another great takeaway exercise.

RUBBER BANDS

Closer

Materials

Different color rubber bands

Directions

- Pass around the rubber bands and ask participants to choose one they can put on their thumb and forefinger and flex.

- When everyone has a rubber band, ask them to do so, flexing it back and forth.

- Ask the participants, "What would happen if this rubber band were left in a drawer for a year and you took it out to use it?" The response you are looking for is, "It would break."

- Tell the participants, "Your mind is like a rubber band. You need to take it out and stretch it every day so it doesn't get dried up and break when you want to use it! Put the rubber band in a special place to remind you to stretch!"

Comment

This exercise puts an emphasis on immediate learning transfer.

SHAPE UP

Closer

Materials

Triangles, circles, squares
Marking pens
Masking tape

Directions

- Divide participants into small groups and give each group a triangle, a circle, a square, a marking pen, and some masking tape.

- Ask them to think about the information learned in the workshop and to record information on the shapes as follows:

    - Triangle—most significant information
    - Circle—information that will stay around for a while
    - Square—information that "squares" with prior training and experiences.

- Ask each group to share their triangles and post them together. Then to the same for the circles and the squares.

Comment

This exercise is a creative way to emphasize the art of communication—fun too!

FINAL WORDS

Closer

Materials

Easel pad paper
Markers of different colors
Masking tape

Directions

- Label one piece of pad paper with "Learning" and another piece with "Words." (Add additional pieces of chart paper depending on the size of the group.)

- Tape the charts on opposite walls in the rooms and provide several different colors of markers for each chart.

- Participants go to the charts and write one thing they learned or reaffirmed on the "Learning" chart paper and one thing they want to say about the training experience on the "Words" chart paper.

Comment

Before everyone leaves, be sure to review what is on both charts with the group. If you used this activity as an Opener ("Learning Words" on page 31), it's a nice way to end and bring the the session full circle.

Geri McArdle, Ph.D. has been a successful human resource manager, educator, and consultant in both the public and private sectors. She was selected as outstanding faculty member of the year in the Department of Business Administration and Management at the Johns Hopkins University. She is currently a fellow at the Philosophy of Education Research Center at Harvard University. She has written a number of books on training and performance improvement and is recognized as a master trainer by the Association for Talent Development (ATD).